G000240517

Published by Ice House Books

Copyright © 2020 Ice House Books

Editor: Zulekhá Afzal
Designer: Kayleigh Hudson
Photography credits overleaf

Ice House Books is an imprint of Half Moon Bay Limited
The Ice House, 124 Walcot Street, Bath, BA1 5BG
www.icehousebooks.co.uk

ISBN 978-1-912867-92-9

Printed in China

SCHOOL of ALCHEMY

Bewitched Baking

ICE HOUSE BOOKS

GRAPHY

o / shutterstock.com

e Coleman / shutterstock.com

rincu / shutterstock.com

o Danil Vitalevich / shutterstock.com

imp / shutterstock.com

enc / shutterstock.com

Dorota / shutterstock.com

0702 / shutterstock.com

nell / shutterstock.com

Mente / shutterstock.com

Zajchikova / shutterstock.com

dra Anschiz / shutterstock.com

Borodin / shutterstock.com

r / shutterstock.com

Haurylik / shutterstock.com

Pustynnikova / shutterstock.com

CONTENTS

MIDNIGHT INCANTATIONS
(Blackberry Cupcakes)

INGREDIENTS

For the cupcakes:

- 150 g (5 oz) blackberries
- 100 g (4 oz) unsalted butter, room temp
- 100 g (4 oz) milk chocolate, broken up
- 225 g (8 oz) self-raising flour
- 175 g (6 oz) golden caster sugar
- 2 tbsp cocoa powder
- 2 free-range eggs
- 100 ml (4 fl oz) boiled water

For the buttercream:

- 100 g (4 oz) unsalted butter, room temp
- 400 g (14 oz) icing sugar
- 1 tsp vanilla extract
- purple food colouring
- 12 blackberries for garnish

Makes: 12 cupcakes
Prep Time: 20 to 30 minutes
Cook Time: 15 minutes

Turn the page for the method.

METHOD

1 Preheat the oven to 180°C/ 160°C fan/Gas 4 and line your cupcake tin with cupcake cases.

2 Put the blackberries in a bowl and roughly crush them with the back of a fork, so there's some juice and they're still a bit chunky.

3 Heat a pan over a medium heat and gently melt the butter and chocolate, stirring occasionally. Take the pan off the heat.

4 Sift the flour into a mixing bowl and add the sugar, cocoa powder and salt.

5 Add the eggs, crushed blackberries, melted butter and chocolate to the dry ingredients, along with the boiled water. Mix until well combined and smooth.

6 Spoon the cake batter into the cupcake cases and bake for 15 minutes. Test they're baked by inserting a skewer – if it comes out clean, they're ready. Leave them to cool a little before transferring them to a wire rack to cool completely.

7 While they're cooling, make your two-tone buttercream. Beat the butter, icing sugar and vanilla extract together in a bowl until light and fluffy. Transfer half the buttercream to another bowl.

8 Add a small amount of the purple food colouring to one bowl of buttercream and mix. The more colouring you add, the stronger the colour will be.

9 Fit a star nozzle into your piping bag ready to create the buttercream swirl. Carefully spoon the natural-coloured buttercream into the piping bag so it sits down one side. Do the same again, adding the purple buttercream to the other side of the piping bag. Twist the top of the piping bag so the buttercream doesn't ooze out the top.

10 When the cupcakes have cooled, pipe a buttercream swirl onto each cupcake and top them with a fresh blackberry to decorate.

UNEARTHLY ROMANCE
(Red Velvet Cupcakes)

INGREDIENTS

For the cupcakes:

- 250 g (9 oz) plain flour
- 2 tsp baking powder
- ½ tsp bicarbonate of soda
- 2 tbsp cocoa powder
- 100 g (4 oz) unsalted butter, room temp
- 200 g (7 oz) caster sugar
- red food colouring
- 2 tsp vanilla extract
- 2 free-range eggs
- 175 ml (6 fl oz) buttermilk
- 1 tsp cider vinegar

For the cream-cheese frosting:

- 500 g (17 oz) icing sugar
- 125 g (4 oz) cream cheese
- 125 g (4 oz) unsalted butter, room temp
- 1 tsp cider vinegar
- red sugar to decorate

Makes: 24 cupcakes
Prep Time: 20 minutes
Extra Time: 20 minutes

Turn the page for the method.

Method

1 Preheat the oven to 170°C/ 150°C fan/Gas 3 and line two cupcake tins with cases.

2 Sift the flour, baking powder, bicarbonate of soda and cocoa powder into a mixing bowl. Mix until combined.

3 In a different mixing bowl, beat the butter and sugar together until light and fluffy. Add some red food colouring and beat it with the butter and sugar – the more colouring you add, the stronger the colour will be. Add the vanilla extract and beat again.

4 Add one spoonful of the dry ingredients, followed by one egg, and mix until combined. Repeat this step then add the rest of the dry ingredients. Mix until combined.

5 Beat in the buttermilk and vinegar, then divide the mixture between the cupcake cases.

6 Bake for approx. 20 minutes or until springy to the touch. Test they're baked by inserting a skewer – if it comes out clean, they're ready.

7 Leave them to cool on a wire rack before decorating.

8 Make the cream-cheese frosting while the cupcakes cool. Sift the icing sugar into a mixing bowl. Add the cream cheese and butter and beat together until combined. Add the vinegar and continue to beat until smooth.

9 Fit a star nozzle into your piping bag ready to create the frosting swirl. Spoon the frosting into the bag, gently squeeze the icing down towards the nozzle, and twist the bag at the top so the frosting doesn't ooze out the top.

10 Once the cupcakes have cooled, swirl the frosting onto each cupcake then sprinkle over the red sugar for decoration. Voilà!

SERPENT'S BREATH
(Matcha Cupcakes)

INGREDIENTS

For the cupcakes:
- 175 g (6 oz) unsalted butter, room temp
- 175 g (6 oz) golden caster sugar
- 3 free-range eggs
- 1 tsp vanilla extract
- 175 g (6 oz) self-raising flour
- ¼ tsp baking powder
- ¼ tsp salt

For the buttercream:
- 175 g (6 oz) unsalted butter, room temp
- 350 g (12 oz) icing sugar
- 1–2 tsp matcha powder

Makes: 12 cupcakes
Prep Time: 15 to 20 minutes
Cook Time: 15 to 20 minutes

METHOD

1 Preheat the oven to 180°C/ 160°C fan/Gas 4 and line a cupcake tin with cupcake cases.

2 Beat the butter and sugar together in a mixing bowl until light and fluffy. Add the eggs and vanilla extract and beat again.

3 In another mixing bowl, sift in the flour, baking powder and salt. Mix well then fold the dry ingredients into the wet ingredients, until combined.

4 Bake for 15–20 minutes or until they're golden on top. Test they're baked by inserting a skewer – if it comes out clean, the cupcakes are ready. Leave them to cool slightly before moving them to a wire rack to finish cooling.

5 While they're cooling, make the buttercream icing. Beat the butter and icing sugar together until very soft. Add the matcha powder and mix until combined.

6 Spoon the buttercream into a piping bag fitted with a star nozzle, and twist the bag at the top so the buttercream doesn't ooze out the top. Pipe your buttercream swirls on the cupcakes, and enjoy.

Speckled Sorcery
(Blueberry Muffins)

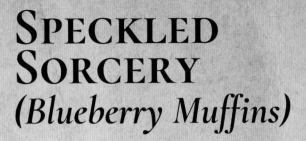

Ingredients

- 100 g (4 oz) unsalted butter, room temp
- 140 g (5 oz) golden caster sugar
- 2 free-range eggs
- 140 g (5 oz) plain yoghurt
- 1 tsp vanilla extract
- 2 tbsp milk
- 250 g (9 oz) plain flour
- 2 tsp baking powder
- 1 tsp bicarbonate of soda
- ¼ tsp salt
- 125 g (4 oz) blueberries

Makes: 12 muffins
Prep Time: 15 to 20 minutes
Cook Time: 20 to 23 minutes

METHOD

1 Preheat the oven to 200°C/
180°C fan/Gas 6 and line a
muffin tin with muffin cases.

2 In a mixing bowl, beat together
the butter and sugar until
light and fluffy. Add the eggs
and beat again, then add the
yoghurt, vanilla extract and
milk. Mix until combined.

3 Sift the flour, baking powder,
bicarbonate of soda and salt
into another bowl and mix.

4 Add the dry ingredients
to the wet ingredients and
mix until combined. Stir in
the blueberries until evenly
distributed throughout the
batter, then spoon the batter
into the muffin cases.

5 Bake for five minutes then
reduce the temperature to
180°C/160°C fan/Gas 4.
Continue to bake for
approximately 15–18 minutes
or until the muffins have risen
and are golden on top. Test
they're baked by inserting a
skewer – if it comes out clean,
they're ready.

6 Leave them to cool slightly
before transferring to a wire
rack to cool completely.
Tuck in!

Truth-Telling Indulgence
(Double Chocolate Cookies)

Ingredients

- 160 g (6 oz) plain flour
- 30 g (1 oz) cocoa powder
- ½ tsp baking powder
- ¼ tsp salt
- 125 g (4 oz) unsalted butter, room temp
- 100 g (4 oz) caster sugar
- 100 g (4 oz) brown sugar

- 1 free-range egg
- 1 tsp vanilla extract
- 170 g (6 oz) chocolate chips

Makes: approx. 18 cookies
Prep Time: 15 minutes
Cook time: 9 to 12 minutes

Method

1 Preheat the oven to 180°C/ 160°C fan/Gas 4 and line a baking sheet with greaseproof paper.

2 Sift the flour into a bowl. Add the cocoa powder, baking powder and salt. Mix well.

3 In a separate mixing bowl, cream together the butter and two sugars until light and fluffy. Add the egg and vanilla extract and beat until combined.

20

4 Add the dry ingredients to the wet ingredients and beat until just combined. Stir in the chocolate chips until evenly distributed in the dough.

5 Take tablespoon-sized amounts of the dough, roll into balls and flatten slightly. Place on the baking tray and make sure to leave space between each cookie, as they will spread.

6 Bake for approximately 9–12 minutes or until they've puffed up a little. Allow the cookies to cool slightly before transferring them to a wire rack to cool completely, or enjoy warm with a cuppa.

DARK PROPHECY
(Dark Chocolate Brownies)

INGREDIENTS

For the brownie:
- 100 g (4 oz) butter, chopped
- 200 g (7 oz) dark chocolate, broken up
- 4 free-range eggs
- 250 g (9 oz) golden caster sugar
- 100 g (4 oz) plain flour
- 1 tsp baking powder
- 30 g (1 oz) cocoa powder

For the decoration:
- 115 g (4 oz) dark chocolate, broken up
- 180 g (6 oz) pomegranate seeds

Makes: 9 to 12 servings
Prep Time: 15 to 20 minutes
Cook Time: 25 to 30 minutes

METHOD

1 Preheat the oven to 180°C/ 160°C fan/Gas 4 and line a square brownie tin with greaseproof paper.

2 Put the chopped butter and broken up chocolate into a microwave-safe bowl and microwave until melted, stirring intermittently. Alternatively, set the bowl over a pan of simmering water and stir until melted. Once melted, set aside and leave to cool.

3 In a mixing bowl, whisk together the eggs and sugar until light and fluffy. Fold in the chocolate mixture.

4 Sift the flour, baking powder and cocoa powder into the bowl. Fold the ingredients together to create your brownie batter.

5 Bake for 25–30 minutes or until cracks appear on the top. Leave to cool slightly before taking the brownie out of the tin and transferring it to a wire rack to cool completely.

6 While it's cooling, add the chocolate for decoration to a heatproof bowl and melt over a pan of simmering water. Drizzle the melted chocolate over the brownie and leave it to set before cutting the brownie into squares. Top with pomegranate seeds and indulge.

OOZING SECRETS
(Jam Doughnuts)

INGREDIENTS

- 160 ml (6 fl oz) warm water
- 7 g (0.2 oz) instant yeast sachet
- 55 g (2 oz) golden caster sugar
- 500 g (18 oz) strong white flour
- pinch of salt
- 100 g (4 oz) unsalted butter, cubed
- 2 free-range eggs
- 2 ltr (70 fl oz) sunflower oil
- icing sugar for coating
- 370 g (13 oz) strawberry jam
  for filling (or your favourite flavour)

Makes: up to 20 doughnuts
Prep Time: 45 to 60 minutes
Cook Time: 30 to 40 minutes
Extra Time: 3 hours

Turn the page for the method.

METHOD

1 Pour the warm water into a jug and add the yeast and one tablespoon of sugar. Give it a stir to dissolve the yeast and sugar – it will froth up slightly.

2 Sift the flour into a large mixing bowl. Add the remaining sugar and the salt, then mix. Add the butter and use your fingertips to rub the butter into the flour mixture, until it resembles breadcrumbs.

3 Mix in the eggs then add the yeast mix. Fold together until a soft dough forms.

4 Lightly flour a work surface and knead the dough until springy, for approximately 10 minutes.

5 Lightly oil a bowl and put the dough inside. Cover and pop the bowl in a warm place for about one hour, or until the dough has doubled in size.

6 When the dough has risen, knead it again for about 3–4 minutes on a lightly floured surface, to knock out the air. Leave it to rest for five minutes.

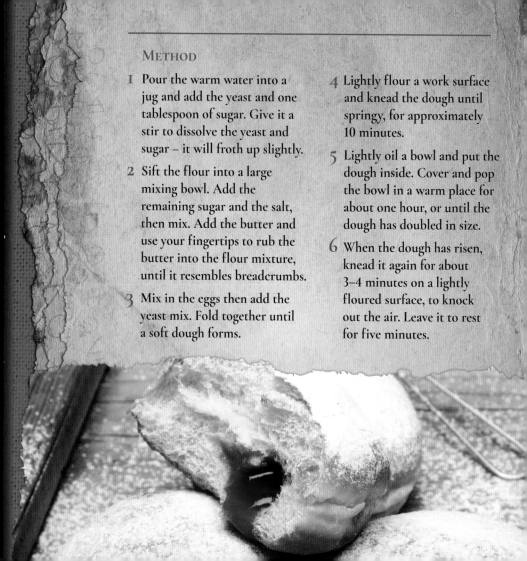

7 To create your individual doughnuts, divide the dough into 20 pieces (or less depending on the size you'd like your doughnuts) and roll them into balls. Lightly oil a few baking sheets and place the balls on the sheets, with enough room between them as they will expand. Loosely cover the balls with a tea towel. Put the balls in a warm place to prove, for approx. 1–2 hours, until they've doubled in size again.

8 Warm a deep, heavy-based pan over a medium heat and partly fill it with sunflower oil. Use a thermometer to heat the oil to 160°C – hot oil can be dangerous so don't leave it unattended.

9 When the oil is the right temperature, gently pick up a doughnut with a lightly floured palette knife and slowly put it into the hot oil.

10 Fry the doughnuts in batches for 3–4 minutes or until golden brown on one side, before flipping them and cooking for another 3–4 minutes on the other side. Remove the doughnuts and roll them in the icing sugar. Set them aside to cool.

11 When the doughnuts have cooled a little, use a skewer or knife to poke a hole into one side of each doughnut that reaches to the centre. Either fill a piping bag or syringe with the jam and generously pipe or syringe the jam into the centre of each doughnut. Mmm!

SILENT WHISPERS
(Pistachio Macarons)

INGREDIENTS

For the maracrons:

- 100 g (4 oz) free-range egg whites
- 100 g (4 oz) caster sugar
- 100 g (4 oz) almond flour
- 100 g (4 oz) icing sugar
- 2 tbsp pistachio paste
- green food colouring

For the filling:

- 100 ml (4 fl oz) double cream
- 250 g (9 oz) white chocolate, broken up
- 2 tbsp pistachio paste
- green food colouring

Makes: up to 30 macarons
Prep Time: 20 to 30 minutes
Cook Time: 13 minutes
Extra time: 20 minutes

Turn the page for the method.

METHOD

1. Preheat the oven to 150°C/ 130°C fan/Gas 2 and line two baking sheets with greaseproof paper.

2. Heat some water in a small pan over a medium heat until it steams. Use a standing mixer to combine the egg whites and sugar, then sit the bowl (of the mixer) over the steaming water to create a double boiler.

3. Whisk together the egg whites and sugar until the sugar melts and the egg whites are white and frothy. Remove the bowl from the heat and put it back on the standing mixer. Whisk on high until stiff peaks form, for approx. 2–3 minutes, to make your Swiss meringue.

4. In another bowl, sift together the almond flour and icing sugar. Add it to the Swiss meringue, along with the pistachio paste and green food colouring.

5. Whisk on a medium setting for 10 seconds then stop the mixer. Using a spatula, gently scoop up some of the batter and try to make a figure eight with the dripping batter, without it breaking. If the batter breaks, whisk it on medium for another 5–10 seconds then try making the figure eight with the dripping batter again.

6. Fit a piping bag with a round nozzle (no bigger than one inch) and spoon the batter into the bag. Pipe small circles onto your baking sheets, leaving space between each macaron half. To remove any air bubbles, gently bang the baking sheets on the kitchen counter two times.

7 Bake for 13 minutes, turning the baking sheets around halfway through baking. Leave the macaron halves to cool completely before taking them off the baking sheets.

8 While the macaron halves are baking and cooling, make your ganache filling. Pour the double cream into a microwave-safe bowl and microwave for 45 seconds. Stir in the white chocolate until it melts into the cream, and add the pistachio paste and green food colouring.

9 Fit a smaller round nozzle into another piping bag and spoon the ganache into the bag. Put the filled bag into the fridge for approximately 20 minutes to harden the ganache slightly.

10 Once the macarons have cooled and the ganache has hardened, pipe the ganache onto half the macarons then sandwich them with another macaron. Try not to eat them all in one go!

CRYSTAL GEMS
(Blueberry Macarons)

INGREDIENTS

For the maracrons:
- 115 g (4 oz) almond flour
- 230 g (8 oz) icing sugar
- 1 tbsp freeze dried blueberry powder
- 145 g (5 oz) free-range egg whites
- 70 g (2 oz) caster sugar
- pinch of salt
- blue food colouring
- blue sugar sprinkles to decorate

For the filling:
- 200 ml (7 fl oz) double cream
- 400 g (14 oz) white chocolate, broken up

Makes: up to 30 macarons
Prep Time: 20 to 30 minutes
Cook Time: 20 to 25 minutes
Extra time: 60 to 90 minutes

Turn the page for the method.

METHOD

1. Line two baking sheets with greaseproof paper.

2. To make the macaron shells, sift the almond flour, icing sugar and blueberry powder into a mixing bowl. Mix together then set aside.

3. Use a standing mixer to whisk the egg whites, sugar, salt and food colouring (the more you add, the stronger the colour will be). Beat for three minutes on medium then increase the speed to medium-high for a further three minutes. Increase the speed a little more for another three minutes, then to high for one minute. The meringue should stick to the whisk when you lift it.

4. Add the dry ingredients to the meringue mixture and gently fold them together. Test the batter is mixed by spooning some of the batter out of the bowl and dropping it back in. It's done if it incorporates with the batter in the bowl again within 20 seconds.

5. Fit a piping bag with a round nozzle (no bigger than one inch) and spoon the batter into the bag. Pipe small circles onto your baking sheets, leaving space between each macaron half. To remove any air bubbles, gently bang the baking sheets on the kitchen counter two times. Leave them to rest for 45–60 minutes.

6 Preheat the oven to 135ºC/ 115ºC fan/Gas 1. Bake for 20–25 minutes, turning the baking sheets around halfway through baking. Leave the macaron halves to cool completely before taking them off the baking sheets.

7 While the macaron halves are baking and cooling, make your ganache filling. Pour the double cream into a microwave-safe bowl and microwave it for 45 seconds. Stir in the white chocolate until it melts into the cream – you could add blue food colouring or leave it as is.

8 Fit a smaller round nozzle into another piping bag and spoon the ganache into the bag. Put the filled bag into the fridge for approximately 20 minutes to harden the ganache slightly.

9 Once the macarons have cooled and the ganache has hardened, pipe the ganache onto half the macarons then sandwich them with another macaron. Sprinkle the sugar sprinkles on top and devour.

Golden Heart
(Custard Tarts)

Ingredients

For the pastry:

- 165 g (6 oz) plain flour
- 25 g (1 oz) ground almonds
- 120 g (4 oz) unsalted butter, chilled and cubed
- 55 g (2 oz) caster sugar
- 1 free-range egg

Makes: 12 tarts
Prep Time: 30 minutes
Cook Time: 30 minutes
Extra Time: 30 minutes

For the filling:

- 700 ml (25 fl oz) whole milk
- 7 free-range egg yolks
- ½ tsp vanilla extract
- 90 g (3 oz) caster sugar
- ground nutmeg for sprinkling
- berries for garnish

Turn the page for the method.

METHOD

1 Begin by making the pastry. In a large mixing bowl, sift in the flour and combine with the ground almonds. Add the chilled butter and rub it in with your fingertips until the mixture looks like breadcrumbs, then add the sugar and stir.

2 Add the egg and use your fingers to combine it with the flour mixture, until a soft dough forms.

3 Transfer the dough to a lightly floured baking sheet and shape it into a ball. Flatten it into a disc with your hands then cover it with a tea towel and refrigerate for 30 minutes.

4 Preheat the oven to 200°C/ 180°C fan/Gas 6.

5 Lightly flour a surface and roll out the pastry. Use an 11 cm fluted cutter to cut out 12 discs. Line a 12-hole muffin tin with the discs and crimp the overlapping edges around the top.

6 Next, make your custard filling. Warm a pan over a medium heat and add the milk. In a large bowl, beat together the egg yolks, vanilla extract and sugar until pale and creamy.

7 Once the milk is warmed through, add it to the egg yolk mixture and stir well. (Little bubbles will appear.)

8 Transfer the custard mixture to a pouring jug then fill each pastry case about two-thirds full, topping them up with any leftover custard. Sprinkle some ground nutmeg on top.

9 Bake for approximately 20–25 minutes until a slight dome appears on the custard. Turn the temperature down after 15 minutes to 180°C/160°C fan/Gas 4.

10 Leave them to cool in the tin for around 30 minutes or until they're firm enough to loosen around the edge with a knife. Carefully transfer the tarts to a wire rack to cool completely. Serve on their own or with some delicious berries.

ENCHANTED TRICKERY
(Blueberry Cheesecake)

INGREDIENTS

- 50 g (2 oz) butter, melted, plus extra for greasing
- 200 g (7 oz) ginger biscuits
- 400 g (14 oz) mascarpone
- 350 g (12 oz) cream cheese
- 125 g (4 oz) caster sugar
- 2 tbsp cornflour
- 1 tsp vanilla essence
- 3 free-range eggs
- zest of 1 small orange, grated
- 300 g (11 oz) blueberries, reserve a handful for garnish
- mint for garnish

Makes: 8 to 12 servings
Prep Time: 10 to 15 minutes
Cook Time: 45 to 60 minutes
Extra Time: 3 to 5 hours

Turn the page for the method.

METHOD

1 Preheat the oven to 180°C/ 160°C fan/Gas 4 and grease a deep, round springform tin with butter.

2 Put the biscuits into a zip close food bag and bash them with a rolling pin until they resemble breadcrumbs. Transfer them to a mixing bowl.

3 Heat a pan over a low-medium heat and add the butter. Gently melt the butter, stirring occasionally. Once melted, pour the butter over the biscuits and mix until combined. Spoon the mixture into the tin and press it down with the back of a spoon so it evenly covers the base. Refrigerate for 10–20 minutes.

4 While the biscuit base is chilling, make the cream cheese mixture. Add the mascarpone, cream cheese, caster sugar, cornflour, vanilla essence, eggs and orange zest to a large bowl. Beat with an electric whisk until combined.

5 Stir the blueberries into the cream cheese mixture (setting a handful aside) until well distributed. Pour the mixture over the biscuit base, spreading it out so it's even.

6 Place the tin on a baking sheet and bake for 45–60 minutes, until the top is golden brown. Open the oven door and leave the cheesecake inside to cool. Once it's cool, remove the cheesecake from the tin and chill it in the fridge, covered, for a few hours.

7 Decorate the cheesecake with the remaining blueberries and some mint. Perfection!

Pumpkin Poison

(Pumpkin Bread)

Makes: 8 to 10 slices
Prep Time: 20 to 25 minutes
Cook Time: 65 to 75 minutes

Ingredients

- 85 g (3 oz) unsalted butter, room temp, plus extra for greasing
- 130 g (5 oz) plain flour, plus extra for greasing
- ½ tsp bicarbonate of soda
- ½ tsp baking powder
- pinch of salt
- ½ tsp ground cloves
- ½ tsp ground cinnamon
- ½ tsp ground nutmeg
- 200 g (7 oz) sugar
- 1 free-range egg
- 200 g (7 oz) pumpkin purée

Turn the page for the method.

METHOD

1 Preheat the oven to 165°C/ 145°C fan/Gas 3. Prepare a loaf tin by greasing it with butter and a dusting of flour.

2 In a mixing bowl, sift in the flour and add the bicarbonate of soda, baking powder, salt, cloves, cinnamon, and nutmeg. Mix well to combine.

3 In a separate mixing bowl, beat together the butter and sugar until just blended. Add the eggs, one at a time, and mix them in until light and fluffy. Add the pumpkin purée and beat again – the mixture may turn a little grainy at this point.

4 Add the dry ingredients to the wet ingredients and mix until well combined.

5 Spoon the loaf batter into the loaf tin and bake for approximately 65–75 minutes or until golden on top. Test it's baked all the way through by inserting a skewer– if it comes out clean, the loaf is ready.

6 Leave to cool slightly before transferring the pumpkin bread to a wire rack to cool completely. Enjoy!

BITTER WITCHCRAFT
(Blood Orange Cake)

INGREDIENTS

- 100 g (4 oz) butter, melted, plus extra for greasing
- 3 tbsp demerara sugar
- 50 ml (2 fl oz) Greek yoghurt
- 1–2 blood oranges, sliced and seeds removed
- 2 free-range eggs
- 140 g (5 oz) caster sugar
- 1 tsp vanilla extract
- 120 g (4 oz) plain flour
- 1 tsp baking powder
- pinch of salt
- zest of 1 blood orange, grated

Makes: 8 slices
Prep Time: 15 to 20 minutes
Cook Time: 30 to 35 minutes

Turn the page for the method.

METHOD

1 Preheat the oven to 175°C/
155°C fan/Gas 4. Prepare a
round, springform cake tin by
greasing the bottom and sides
with butter and sprinkling over
the demerara sugar.

2 Warm a pan over a medium
heat and gently melt the butter.
Stir in the yoghurt then set it
aside to cool.

3 Place the blood orange slices
at the bottom of the cake tin
in a single layer.

4 In a mixing bowl, beat together
the eggs, sugar and vanilla
extract until pale and fluffy.

5 In another large bowl, sift in
the flour, baking powder and
salt and mix to combine.
Add the egg mixture to the
dry ingredients and stir them
until combined. Pour in the
melted butter and yoghurt
and add the zest. Stir until
the batter is smooth.

6 Pour the cake batter into
the cake tin, over the blood
orange slices.

7 Bake until the cake is
golden brown on top, for
approximately 30–35 minutes.
Check it's baked by inserting
a skewer into the centre of the
cake – if it comes out clean,
the cake is ready.

8 Leave to cool a little in the tin
before turning the cake upside
down onto a wire rack to cool
completely. It's time to tuck
into a slice (or two!).

CONJURED COMFORTS
(Bread & Butter Pudding)

INGREDIENTS

- 250 ml (9 fl oz) whole milk
- 300 ml (11 fl oz) double cream
- 3 free-range eggs
- 1 free-range egg yolk
- 3 tbsp golden caster sugar
- 1 tsp vanilla extract
- 8–10 slices of white bread
- 50 g (2 oz) butter, room temp,
  plus extra for greasing
- 75 g (3 oz) sultanas,
  zest of ½ a lemon, grated
- 2 tbsp demerara sugar

Makes: 6 to 8 servings
Prep Time: 20 minutes
Cook Time: 35 to 40 minutes
Extra Time: 30 minutes

Turn the page for the method.

METHOD

1 Preheat the oven to 180°C/160°C fan/Gas 4 and lightly grease an ovenproof dish (20 cm x 25 cm x 5 cm) with butter.

2 Begin by making your custard. Heat a pan over a medium heat and add the milk and cream, bringing it to just below the boiling point.

3 In a jug, whisk together the eggs, egg yolk and sugar. Once the milk mixture is warmed through, pour it into the jug with the egg mixture and add the vanilla extract. Stir until smooth.

4 Butter both sides of the bread slices and cut them into triangles. Place half the bread triangles in the bottom of the dish with a slight overlap.

5 Combine the sultanas and lemon zest in a bowl and sprinkle half the mixture over the bread.

6 Lay the remaining bread triangles on the top and sprinkle over the rest of the sultanas and lemon zest mix.

7 Pour the homemade custard over the top and set the pudding aside to soak for at least 30 minutes. Once it's soaked, sprinkle over the demerara sugar.

8 Bake for 35–40 minutes or until it's golden brown on top and looks as though it has puffed up.

9 Allow to cool a little then serve and enjoy.

SWEET RUBY
(Cherry Pie)

INGREDIENTS

For the pastry:

- 350 g (12 oz) plain flour, extra for dusting
- 150 g (5 oz) unsalted butter, cold and diced
- 100 g (4 oz) caster sugar
- 50 g (2 oz) ground almonds
- 2 free-range egg yolks
- dash of cold milk
- 1 free-range egg, for brushing

For the filling:

- 1 kg (35 oz) fresh red cherries
- juice of 1 lemon
- 2 tbsp cornflour
- 100 g (4 oz) caster sugar
- 1 tsp vanilla extract

Makes: 6 to 8 servings
Prep Time: 20 to 30 minutes
Cook Time: 30 to 35 minutes
Extra Time: 30 minutes

Turn the page for the method.

METHOD

1 Begin by making the pie pastry. Add the flour and diced butter to a bowl and rub them together with your fingertips, until they resemble crumbs.

2 Add the sugar, ground almonds and egg yolks. Knead the ingredients together until a dough forms. Add a dash of cold milk if it needs a little help to bind together.

3 Cover the bowl and pop it in the fridge to chill for at least 30 minutes.

4 While the dough is chilling, make the cherry filling. Pit the cherries then add them to a pan with the lemon juice, cornflour, caster sugar and vanilla extract.

5 Gently stir the ingredients over a medium heat for approximately 15 minutes or until the sauce has thickened. Remove from the heat and leave to cool completely.

6 Preheat the oven to 200°C/ 180°C fan/Gas 6. Put a baking sheet in the oven to warm.

7 Lightly flour a surface and roll out about two-thirds of the chilled pastry. Once rolled out, gently lift the pastry and use it to line a fluted tart tin. Carefully press it into the sides of the tin then fill the pastry case with the cherry filling.

8 Roll out the remaining pastry to create a pie lid. Top the pie with the lid and crimp the edges to seal it. Whisk up the egg and brush it over the pastry.

9 Put the tart tin onto the hot baking sheet and bake for approx. 30–35 minutes or until the top is golden brown and the filling is bubbling. Allow the pie to rest for 10 minutes before serving hot.

CRUMBLING MAGIC
(Apple Crumble)

INGREDIENTS

For the filling:
- 1 kg (35 oz) Bramley apples
- pinch of sugar
- 1 tbsp water

Makes: 6 to 8 servings
Prep Time: 20 to 30 minutes
Cook time: 30 to 40 minutes

For the crumble:
- 100 g (4 oz) plain flour
- 75 g (3 oz) butter, room temp
- 50 g (2 oz) rolled oats
- 100 g (4 oz) demerara sugar

METHOD

1 Preheat the oven to 200°C/ 180°C fan/Gas 6.

2 Prepare the apples by cutting them into quarters, removing the cores then slicing each quarter into two.

3 Heat a pan over a medium heat and add the apples. Sprinkle over a little sugar and add the water. Poach the apples for approx. five minutes until they begin to soften.

4 Pour the apple mixture into a shallow pie dish and spread it out so it covers the bottom.

5 To make the crumble, add the flour and butter to a bowl and rub them together with your fingertips, until the mixture resembles breadcrumbs.

6 Add the oats and sugar and stir them in until combined. Carefully pour the crumble mixture into the baking dish, over the apples, and gently spread them so there's an even covering.

7 Bake for approximately 30 minutes or until the crumble is golden brown and crisp. Allow to cool a little before serving.